The 50 State GEMS & MINERALS

A Guidebook for Aspiring Geologists

Schiffer **Kids**™

4880 Lower Valley Road, Atglen, PA 19310

YINAN WANG

This book is dedicated to my dear wife, Heather, who embraces my love of rocks. —Yinan Wang

"Schiffer Kids" logo is a trademark of Schiffer Publishing, Ltd.
Amelia logo is a trademark of Schiffer Publishing, Ltd.

Designed by Danielle D. Farmer
Cover design by Danielle D. Farmer
Maps by Jane Levy
Type set in Rancher BT/Vag Rounded/Optima

ISBN: 978-0-7643-5995-8
Printed in India
Published by Schiffer Kids
An imprint of Schiffer Publishing, Ltd.
4880 Lower Valley Road
Atglen, PA 19310
Phone: (610) 593-1777; Fax: (610) 593-2002
E-mail: Info@schifferbooks.com
Web: www.schifferbooks.com

For our complete selection of fine books on this and related subjects, please visit our website at www.schifferbooks.com. You may also write for a free catalog.

Schiffer Publishing's titles are available at special discounts for bulk purchases for sales promotions or premiums. Special editions, including personalized covers, corporate imprints, and excerpts, can be created in large quantities for special needs. For more information, contact the publisher.

We are always looking for people to write books on new and related subjects. If you have an idea for a book, please contact us at proposals@schifferbooks.com.

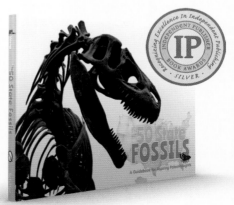

THE 50 STATE FOSSILS, A GUIDEBOOK FOR ASPIRING PALEONTOLOGISTS

Yinan Wang
Illustrations by Jane Levy
978-0-7643-5557-8
10"x7" | 72 pp. | 168 images
$18.99

This kids' guidebook explores each state's official fossil. More than 100 illustrations and photographs bring ancient history to life, from the Basilosaurus whale of Alabama to the Knightia fish of Wyoming. A fun guide for young fossil enthusiasts, it has a comprehensive yet easy-to-read format.

CONTENTS

INTRODUCTION

Minerals and gemstones have always been a part of us. Minerals physically make up much of what we are and what is around us. They provide nutrients we need for our bodies while also providing the components of everything we use in our daily lives: our electronics, vehicles, houses, etc. Gemstones are treasures that we carry around as jewelry, and we consider them of value. Minerals and gems are important parts of us, and this book will explore those that have become state gems and minerals.

Amethyst, a variety of the mineral quartz

WHAT ARE MINERALS AND GEMS?

As defined by the International Mineralogical Association: "A mineral is an element or a chemical compound that is normally crystalline and that has been formed as a result of geological processes." This means that for something to be considered a mineral, it must meet the following standards:

Be an element or chemical compound:

Everything around us is made up of atoms of elements. Minerals can be either a single element or a defined compound of elements. For example, gold is a mineral and an element. It is represented by the chemical formula Au; quartz is a mineral and is a compound represented by the chemical formula SiO_2.

Be normally crystalline:

The atoms of a mineral need to be in an orderly arrangement; usually this is a three-dimensional structure that eventually forms

An assortment of faceted gemstones

Fluorite, a mineral

Amber, a fossil resin, not a mineral

a crystal. This also means that in general a mineral is solid at room temperature. There are some exceptions, such as mercury and ice.

Be formed as a result of a geological process:

A mineral must have been formed without human intervention or from a biological process. Crystals that people grow are not minerals. Shells formed by an animal are not officially recognized as minerals.

Currently new minerals are proposed to and voted on by the International Mineralogical Association, which was established in 1958 to examine and standardize minerals. At the time of this writing there are more than 5,400 minerals. About 100 new minerals are found and defined every year. The accepted definition of "mineral" changes every few decades, so some minerals formed biologically used to be accepted but were then rejected later. The definition of what is a mineral could be redefined in the future and more minerals will be added.

A gemstone (or gem) is a mineral or other similar substance that is attractive and has been cut or polished to be worn in jewelry or shown off. The definition of gemstones is much less strict than that of minerals, and many gemstones are made from organic substances (such as amber and pearls), or even from manmade materials (such as lab grown diamonds). Gemstones are usually cut or polished to make them more attractive, and gemstones that haven't been worked are usually called rough, raw, or uncut.

Side note: In geology, aside from minerals and gemstones, there are also rocks. A rock can be made from a single mineral or can be made from a variety of minerals. A rock can also contain organic remains such as fossils

HOW DO MINERALS FORM?

Minerals are formed when atoms join together to form an orderly structure with the same chemical formula throughout, usually as a crystal. This can occur in a number of ways:

Quartz in a cavity

Minerals (quartz, muscovite, microcline) formed in slow-cooling pegmatite rock

THE COOLING OF MAGMA

Deep in the Earth there is a lot of heat and pressure—so much that rocks melt into a substance called magma. When magma cools, minerals crystallize from the elements within the hot liquid.

THE EVAPORATION OF WATER

As water carrying dissolved minerals evaporates, the minerals become more concentrated and start forming crystals. Halite (salt) is one of the most common minerals that forms this way.

THE COOLING OF WATER

Water can carry a lot of elements and dissolved minerals. These dissolved minerals can crystallize as the water cools. Often, water cooling in cavities (holes in rock) will form geodes filled with crystals.

Halite from California

Pseudomorph where copper replaced aragonite

MINERAL CLASSIFICATION

To help organize minerals, professional mineralogists have classified minerals into ten categories:

1. **Elements:** Minerals that are single elements. Gold, silver, and diamond (carbon) are examples.

2. **Sulfides:** Minerals that contain sulfur as the anion (a negatively charged atom that positively charged atoms attach to). Pyrite and galena are examples.

OTHER WAYS

While these are the most-common ways that minerals form, there are others. Chemical interactions can occur that result in the combination of atoms to form minerals. Various chemical and geological processes can exchange the atoms in one mineral for those of another while preserving the original shape, resulting in what's called a pseudomorph. Minerals can also precipitate out of hot gases instead of liquids. While not formally recognized as minerals, many organisms do form minerals, such as aragonite in bones and teeth.

Gold, an element and a mineral

Pyrite, a sulfide mineral

Rhodochrosite, a carbonate mineral

3. Halogenides (also called halides): Minerals that contain a halogen element as the anion. Fluorite and halite are examples.

4. Oxides: Minerals that contain oxygen as the anion. Corundum (ruby and sapphire) is an example.

5. Carbonates: Minerals that contain carbonate (CO_3) as the anion. Calcite is an example.

6. Borates: Minerals that contain borate (BO_3) as the anion. Borax is an example.

7. Sulfates: Minerals that contain the sulfate SO_4 as the anion. Celestine and gypsum are examples.

8. Phosphates: Minerals that contain phosphate (PO_4) as the anion. Turquoise is an example.

9. Silicates: This group of minerals contain SiO_4 and makes up 90% of the Earth's crust. Examples include beryl, tourmalines, and the garnet group.

10. Organic compounds: Minerals that contain certain organic compounds. Some of these are accepted minerals, while others are not.

These are the main classifications, but there are further classifications under many of these sections.

A specimen of opal found by the author

ROCK HUNTING

Rock hunting is a classic hobby that involves looking for and collecting minerals and gemstones. The best way to get introduced to rock hunting is to join a local rock-collecting club and attend their field trips. Minerals are found in every state, but not everywhere in a state. Clubs and other groups can help provide access to collecting sites, guidelines for best practices for collecting, and tips on staying safe. In many states there are pay-to-dig sites where visitors can hunt for gems and minerals on a property; these places will often provide instruction and some equipment to help visitors. Occasionally, museums and colleges will also have field trips to places with interesting minerals.

Clubs and other groups can also help keep mineral hunters updated about local, state, and federal laws on mineral collecting. There are rules regarding where and what a person can collect. Mineral collecting is illegal in national parks and national monuments. Laws about collecting on other federal and state land vary greatly. Mineral hunters must always ask permission before collecting on private land. Laws are also constantly changing, so always check with the authorities of a place before planning a trip. Many people in clubs will also help a collector identify their finds. A person does not have to be a geologist to hunt for minerals, but mineral collecting is a good way to get started in becoming a future geologist.

OTHER THINGS TO KNOW ABOUT GEMS AND MINERALS

There is much more to know about gems and minerals than can be written into this book, but there are a few things that will come in handy for this reading.

You can do your own research to learn more:

Precious versus semiprecious: Historically, gemstones have been separated into categories such as precious (diamond, ruby, sapphire, and emerald) and semiprecious (all others), but this categorization has become less common today.

Mohs scale: Many minerals are ranked by their hardness on what's known as the Mohs scale of hardness. Minerals on this scale are ranked 1 through 10, with 10 being the hardest. It means that a mineral with a higher number can scratch one with a lower number. The common minerals used on this are (1) talc, (2) gypsum, (3) calcite, (4) fluorite, (5) apatite, (6) orthoclase feldspar, (7) quartz, (8) topaz, (9) corundum, and (10) diamond.

Crystal structures: Most minerals form crystals that follow specific repeated arrangements of their atoms. There are specific class- ifications, but this book will describe the more common shapes crystals will form.

Groups, varieties, and gemstone names: Often there is a group name for minerals, and then one for more-specific mineral names. For example, the garnet group has many minerals with the same structure, including almandine, spessartine, and grossular. Each of these minerals can commonly be called a garnet. There are also a variety of names where a mineral has been given different names depending on the color or trace element. For example, both amethyst and citrine are varieties of the mineral quartz. Further, agate is a variety of chalcedony, which is itself a variety of the mineral quartz. There are also gemstone names that were created over the ages; for example, peridot is the gem name for the olivine group mineral forsterite.

Fluorescence: An interesting property of some minerals is fluorescence. This means they emit bright, unique colors when an ultraviolet light is shone on them. Those minerals absorb energy from ultraviolet light and release light in color ranges that we can see.

A diamond crystal from Arkansas

Rock showing fluorescence under UV and normal light

WHY STATE GEMS AND MINERALS?

States designate official symbols to recognize and celebrate important cultural and natural objects of that state. Some of the more common state symbols include state flags and state seals, but there are often also state flowers, state birds, state songs, and many other symbols. Designating a state gem or mineral can bring attention to and celebrate those symbols, potentially increasing tourism and business while encouraging an interest in the field of geology. While every state has minerals and many states produce gemstones, not every state has officially designated gems and minerals. At the time of this writing, there are twenty-four states with official minerals and thirty-five states with official gems. Many states also have related geologic symbols, such as state stones, rocks, and crystals. If a state does not have a state mineral or a state gem, the citizens of that state can work to get one designated.

HOW A STATE GEM OR MINERAL GETS DESIGNATED

1. Someone notices his or her state does not have a state gem or mineral.

2. Either individually or as a group, the citizens of that state research local gems and minerals and pick one to propose to be officially designated. This is often done by classrooms of students, hobbyists, or even industry groups.

3. The individual or group contacts elected representatives of the state and works with them on writing a bill designating the state gem or mineral.

4. The bill goes through the state legislative process and is voted on, usually by both the House and Senate of that state.

5. If the bill makes it through the legislature and is signed by the governor, the state gem or mineral is then designated by law.

Alabama

State Capital
State gems may be found in this area
State minerals may be found in this area

Montgomery

Rough star blue quartz
from Alabama

GEM:
STAR BLUE QUARTZ

(pronounced ka-wort-s)
Chemical Formula: SiO_2 with trace elements
Star blue quartz was designated the state gem in 1990.

Blue is a rare color for quartz, as is the ability to have star-shaped patterns, which is why star blue quartz from Alabama is special. Found in a small area of eastern Alabama, this type of quartz is anhedral, meaning it does not have crystal faces, but rather is in a chunky mass. It gets its blue color from inclusions of other minerals such as rutile and ilmenite. When polished, it can show an asterism (a star shape) with 4 or 12 lines due to the mineral inclusions.

MINERAL:
HEMATITE – RED IRON ORE

(pronounced hee-ma-tight)
Chemical Formula: Fe_2O_3
Hematite was designated the state mineral in 1967.

Hematite from Red Hill, Alabama

Hematite is a mineral that contains a lot of iron, and in Alabama it is also referred to as "red iron ore." The presence of hematite and other resources around the city of Birmingham helped turn it into an industrial city as the hematite was mined for iron. More than 375 million tons of iron ore have been mined in Alabama.

Sidenote: Marble was declared the state rock in 1969.

GEM:
JADE

(pronounced Jae-d)
Mineral name: nephrite
(pronounced neh-fright)
Chemical Formula:
$Ca_2(Mg, Fe)_5Si_8O_{22}(OH)_2$
Jade was designated the state
gem in 1968.

Slab of nephrite jade from Alaska

Nephrite jade cabochon
from Alaska

Juneau

★ State Capital

State gems may be found in this area

State minerals may be found in this area

Jade is the gem name for two minerals: jadeite and nephrite. Alaskan jade is the mineral nephrite, which presents as a variety of dark green colors. Much of Alaska's jade comes from western Alaska along the Kobuk River. Ancient jade artifacts made by indigenous people have also been found throughout the region.

MINERAL:
GOLD

(pronounced gohld)
Chemical Formula: Au
Gold was designated the state mineral in 1968.

Gold nugget
from Alaska

Gold is measured using what is called a troy ounce; it is a little heavier than a normal ounce. Gold has played an important role in Alaska's history, as tens of thousands of people traveled to Alaska during "gold rushes" in the late 1800s hoping to strike it rich. Since then more than 47 million troy ounces of gold have been mined in the state. The "Alaska Centennial Nugget" is the largest gold nugget ever found in Alaska; weighing 294 troy ounces, or 20 pounds, it is about the size of a grapefruit and was found in 1998.

Arizona

State Capital
State gems may be found in this area
State minerals may be found in this area

Phoenix

GEM:
TURQUOISE

(pronounced ter-coiz)
Chemical Formula:
$CuAl_6(PO_4)_4(OH)_8 \cdot 4H_2O$
Turquoise was designated the state gem in 1974.

Turquoise cabochon from
Kingman, Arizona

MINERAL:
WULFENITE

(pronounced wool-fen-night)
Chemical Formula: $PbMoO_4$
Wulfenite was designated the state mineral in 2017.

Wulfenite crystal from
Yuma County,
Arizona

Turquoise is a mineral that comes in various shades of blue and is considered a secondary mineral: it is formed by the weathering of other minerals, such as copper. In Arizona, turquoise is found in and near several copper mines. It has been used in jewelry and artifacts by Native Americans for hundreds of years. Individual deposits of turquoise tend to be very distinctive, and it's possible to figure out which mine a piece came from on the basis of its color and patterns.

Wulfenite is a mineral with flat, tabular crystals and has a color ranging from yellow to red. It is occasionally found while mining for metals such as silver or lead. In Arizona some of the most famous specimens come from the Red Cloud mine, which started as a silver mine in 1878 but later was operated just to dig wulfenite crystals. A wulfenite from the Red Cloud Mine was featured on a US postage stamp in 1992.

GEM:
DIAMOND

(pronounced DIE-mund)
Chemical Formula: **C**
Diamond was designated the state gem in 1967.

A diamond from Arkansas

Little Rock

★ State Capital

State gems may be found in this area

State minerals may be found in this area

Diamonds are precious gemstones composed of carbon and have been used as gemstones for hundreds of years. Arkansas's first specimens were discovered in 1906, near the town of Murfreesboro, in the remains of an ancient volcanic pipe. In 1972, the location became Crater of Diamonds State Park, where people can pay a fee to look for diamonds. More than 600 diamonds are found each year by visitors. The largest diamond found in the United States, nicknamed the "Uncle Sam" and weighing 40.23 carats (8.05 grams), was discovered in the crater in 1924.

MINERAL:
QUARTZ

(pronounced ka-wort-s)
Chemical Formula: **SiO₂**
Quartz was designated the state mineral in 1967.

Quartz crystal from Arkansas

Quartz is a very common mineral and can often be found in hexagonal crystal form. One of the best sources of quartz crystals in the United States is the Ouachita Mountains of Arkansas, which have been mined for clear quartz crystals for more than 150 years. While common quartz may be found throughout the state, there are several mines in the Ouachita Mountains region that allow visitors to dig their own clear quartz crystals for a fee.

note: Bauxite was designated the state rock in 1967.

California

Sacramento

★ State Capital

State gems may be found in this area

State minerals may be found in this area

GEM:
BENITOITE

(pronounced ben-NEAT-oh-ite)
Chemical Formula: $BaTi(Si_3O_9)$
Benitoite was designated the state gem in 1985.

A benitoite crystal on matrix from California

A faceted benitoite gemstone

Benitoite is one of the rarest minerals on Earth—rarer than diamonds—with all of the gem-quality material coming from a site in the San Benito Mountains of California. It forms deep-blue triangular crystals with optical properties that make cut gems of benitoite as bright as diamonds. Gem-quality benitoite crystals are very difficult to find, and most cut specimens end up being less than a carat in weight.

MINERAL:
GOLD

(pronounced gold)
Chemical Formula: Au
Gold was designated the state mineral in 1965.

The discovery of gold near Sutter's Mill in 1848 led to the California Gold Rush, which brought 300,000 people to the territory looking for gold and fortune. Many large gold nuggets have been found in California, with the largest being a 1,593-troy-ounce nugget (109 pounds) found in 1869. More than 100 million troy ounces of gold has been mined in California—more than any other state in the United States.

A gold nugget from California

Side note: Serpentine was designated the state rock in 1965.

GEM:
AQUAMARINE

(pronounced awh-kwuh-muh-REEN)
Chemical Formula: ***Beryl— Be₃Al₂Si₆O₁₈***

$$Beryl—Be_3Al_2Si_6O_{18}$$

Aquamarine was designated the state gem in 1971.

Aquamarine crystal from Mount Antero

Aquamarine is the blue form of the mineral beryl. Like other beryl crystals, it forms hexagonal crystals, but impurities of iron give aquamarine beautiful shades of blue. In Colorado, aquamarine crystals measuring up to 7 inches long are famously found on Mount Antero and nearby Mount White. With a height of 14,276 feet, Mount Antero is a difficult place to look for gems because of the thinner air, lightning storms, and rockslides.

Faceted aquamarine from Mount Antero

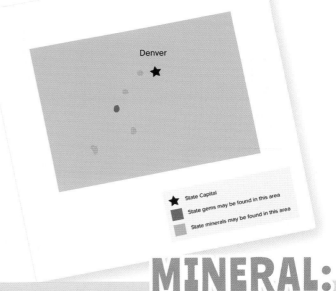

Denver

State Capital
State gems may be found in this area
State minerals may be found in this area

MINERAL:
RHODOCHROSITE

(pronounced row-doe-CROW-site)
Chemical Formula: ***MnCO₃***

$$MnCO_3$$

Rhodochrosite was designated the state mineral in 2002.

Rhodochrosite is a manganese carbonate mineral that forms in shades of red. The world's most beautiful rhodochrosite crystals were found at the Sweet Home Mine near the town of Alma, Colorado. The Sweet Home Mine began as a silver mine in 1872, and the rhodochrosite crystals were at first ignored until later becoming highly valued. The "Alma King" was found in the Sweet Home Mine in 1992; measuring 6.5 inches across, it is considered by many to be the finest rhodochrosite crystal in the world.

Rhodochrosite from the Sweet Home Mine

ide note:

Yule marble was designated the state rock in 2004.

Connecticut

Hartford

★ State Capital

State gems may be found in this area

State minerals may be found in this area

Faceted heliodor from
Connecticut

GEM:
CONNECTICUT
does not have a state gem

Connecticut does not have a state gem but has several minerals that are good candidates, including quartz, tourmalines, and garnets. One excellent candidate is the yellow form of beryl called heliodor (pronounced HE-lee-oh-door). Gem-quality heliodor, or golden beryl, was mined at the Roebling Mine near New Milford for a number of years.

Almandine garnet from
Roxbury, Connecticut

MINERAL:
GARNET
(pronounced GAR-net)
Chemical Formula: Garnet Group, most notably Almandine (pronounced ALL-mon-deen) $Fe_3Al_2Si_3O_{12}$
The garnet was designated the state gem in 1977.

Garnets are a group of silicate minerals that all have similar chemical formulas but with different elements. In Connecticut, the most popular garnets are almandine, which contain iron and aluminum and generally form round crystals with dark-red colors. They can be found in metamorphic rock, which is present throughout much of the state.

Side note:

Marble was declared the state rock in 1969.

Yellow beryl in matrix from Connecticut

GEM:
DELAWARE
does not have a state gem

Schorl tourmaline from
Delaware

Delaware does not have a state gem but has several minerals that are good candidates. Almost all the potential gem minerals are found in the northern tip of the state—called the Piedmont region—while most of the rest of the state is within the Coastal Plain, made of sedimentary rocks. Red almandine garnets are found in parts of the Piedmont region. Black-colored tourmaline crystals called schorl are also present in the Piedmont.

Dover

★ State Capital
State gems may be found in this area
State minerals may be found in this area

MINERAL:
SILLIMANITE
(pronounced SILL-leh-man-ite)
Chemical Formula: Al_2SiO_5
Sillimanite was designated the state mineral in 1977.

Sillimanite from Delaware

Sillimanite is a mineral that forms at temperatures above 1,022 degrees Fahrenheit and can be found in metamorphic rocks. It usually appears as long, thin crystals with white or tan colors, sometimes with many crystals connected together, looking like fibers. Entire boulders of it are found in Brandywine Springs and parts of New Castle County.

Florida

Tallahassee

★ State Capital

State gems may be found in this area

State minerals may be found in this area

Moonstone from Sri Lanka

GEM:
MOONSTONE

Orthoclase
(pronounced OR-thuh-clays)
Chemical Formula: $KAlSi_3O_8$
and occasionally plagioclase
(pronounced PLAH-ge-o-clays)
feldspar $(Na,Ca)AlSi_3O_8$
Moonstone was designated the state
gem in 1970.

Oddly enough, moonstone is not found in Florida but was designated the state gem because the Apollo missions that sent humans to the moon were launched from Florida. Moonstone itself is a gemstone that usually has a blue or white shimmering effect to it, often in the form of a "cat's eye." It is usually a gem variety of the mineral orthoclase feldspar but can also be from plagioclase feldspar.

MINERAL:
FLORIDA
does not have a state mineral

Florida does not have a state mineral, but even though the state is mostly sedimentary rock, it does have an assortment of minerals, including the chalcedony variety of quartz, dolomite, gypsum, and others. One notable mineral is calcite, because one of the popular fossils from Florida is a fossilized clamshell filled with calcite crystals.

Calcite in a fossil clam
from Florida

Side note: Agatized coral was designated the state stone in 1979.

GEM:
QUARTZ

(pronounced ka-wort-s)
Chemical Formula: SiO_2
Quartz was designated the state gem in 1976.

Faceted amethyst
from the Jackson's
Crossroads Mine

Quartz is a common mineral, but nice quartz crystals are uncommon. Georgia has not only nice quartz crystals but also an exceptional purple variety of quartz called amethyst. The Jackson's Crossroads Mine in Wilkes County has been producing beautiful amethyst crystals that are prized for their deep color and clarity. Specimens from the mine have been displayed in museums around the world.

Georgia

Atlanta

★ State Capital
State gems may be found in this area
State minerals may be found in this area

MINERAL:
STAUROLITE

(pronounced STAR-o-light)
Chemical Formula: $Fe^{2+}_2Al_9Si_4O_{23}(OH)$
Staurolite was designated the state mineral in 1976.

Staurolite fairy cross
from Georgia

Staurolite is a mineral that can be found in metamorphic rocks. Occasionally two crystals form from a shared point, resulting in intersecting shapes known as "fairy crosses." There are many folktales about how fairy crosses form, and many people also believe they provide good luck. Some of the best staurolite fairy crosses are found in Fannin County in northern Georgia.

Hawaii

Honolulu

★ State Capital

■ State gems may be found in this area

■ State minerals may be found in this area

Black coral from Hawaii

Polished black coral from Hawaii

MINERAL:
HAWAII
does not have a state mineral

GEM:
BLACK CORAL

(pronounced CORE-uhl)
Organic gemstone—Antipatharia (pronounced anti-PATH-area) order
Black coral was designated the state gem of Hawaii in 1987.

Black coral is not a rock but is formed by a living organism and therefore is an organic gemstone. Corals are colonies of marine animals of the class Anthozoa. They colonize surfaces as individual polyps before forming hard exoskeletons out of calcium carbonate. Black coral is a group of coral that forms treelike branches. There are many rules protecting black corals, but some are legally harvested and polished into dark gemstones.

Hawaii does not have a state mineral; however, because of the volcanic history of the islands, one of the minerals that can be found is forsterite (pronounced FOR-ster-rite) from the olivine (pronounced OLIVE-een) group. Forsterite is also known as the gemstone peridot. Magma carrying forsterite erupts onto the surface as lava, which solidifies into volcanic rock. When the volcanic rock is weathered or is broken up, olivine forsterite crystals are released. Hawaii actually has a beach with green sand (Papakōlea) that gets its color from large quantities of the tiny crystals.

Forsterite olivine sand from Hawaii

GEM:
STAR GARNET

(pronounced GAR-net)
Chemical Formula: Almandine $(Fe_3Al_2Si_3O_{12})$ and Pyrope $(Mg_3Al_2(SiO_4)_3)$ (pronounced pie-rope)
Star garnet was designated the state gem in 1967.

Garnets from Idaho

Star garnets are garnets that possess asterism, an effect where a polished gem has several lines forming a "star" when one is looking at a stone from a certain angle. Star garnets are extremely rare but can be found in northern Idaho. One popular site where visitors can hunt for their own star garnets for the price of a permit is the Emerald Creek Garnet Area of the Idaho Panhandle National Forest.

Polished star garnets from Idaho

Boise

★ State Capital
State gems may be found in this area
State minerals may be found in this area

MINERAL:
IDAHO
does not have a state mineral

Idaho does not have a state mineral, but there are a variety of minerals throughout the state, including vivianite (pronounced VIV-ee-en-ite), quartz, epidote (pronounced EH-peh-dote), and others. One of the interesting minerals from Idaho is opal from near the town of Spencer, which calls itself the "Opal Capital of America." In the Spencer area, opal fills cavities in volcanic rhyolite, and rare forms of opal such as pink opal and star opals (opals with asterism) have been found there. A lot of the opal has beautiful flashes of color that make for great gemstones.

Polished opal from Idaho

Illinois

Springfield ★

★ State Capital

State gems may be found in this area

State minerals may be found in this area

Faceted fluorite
from Illinois

Faceted fluorite
from Illinois

GEM:
ILLINOIS
does not have a state gem

Illinois does not have a state gem. While it does have a variety of minerals, its state mineral, fluorite, would actually make for the best gemstone. Even though it is only a 4 on the Mohs scale of hardness, fluorite from Illinois comes in a variety of rich purple and yellow colors with great clarity.

MINERAL:
FLUORITE
(pronounced FLOOR-rite)
Chemical Formula: CaF_2
Fluorite was designated the state mineral in 1965.

Yellow fluorite
from Illinois

Purple flourite
from Illinois

Fluorite is a mineral that forms cubes and octahedral crystals, often with great clarity and a variety of colors depending on the trace elements. In Illinois, 150 million years ago, hot water containing fluorine seeped into limestone, which contains calcium. This caused some of the rocks to dissolve and crystals of fluorite to form out of those elements. Fluorite was mined for industrial purposes in Illinois, and many fantastic crystals were found as a result.

GEM:
INDIANA
does not have a
state gem

A rare diamond from
Indiana

A calcite crystal from
Indiana

Indianapolis

★

★ State Capital
State gems may be found in this area
State minerals may be found in this area

Indiana does not have a state gem, but diamonds could possibly qualify. Diamonds are crystals made of an arrangement of carbon atoms that make them extremely hard. The first diamond found in the United States was actually found in Ellettsville, Indiana. To date, at least thirty-eight diamonds have been found in the state, with the largest being the "Stanley Diamond," which was found in Morgan County in 1900 and weighted 4⅞ carats. The diamonds probably originated in Canada and were carried into the state by glaciers during the ice ages.

Gold from Indiana

MINERAL:

INDIANA
does not have a state mineral

While Indiana does not have a state mineral, calcite and gold may be good candidates. Calcite (pronounced CAL-site) is a carbonate mineral with the formula $CaCO_3$, and many calcite crystals are found throughout the state in limestone, with many pockets of calcite crystals found during limestone mining. Gold is also found in Indiana, and, like diamonds, it was probably brought to the state by glaciers. Gold panning is a popular hobby in the state, and gold has been found in most of the state.

de note:

Salem limestone was designated the
state stone in 1971

Iowa

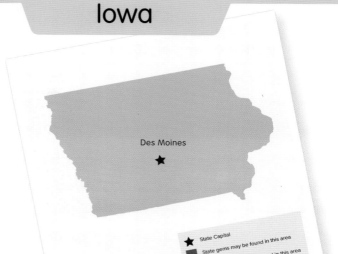

Des Moines

★ State Capital
State gems may be found in this area
State minerals may be found in this area

An agate from Iowa

GEM:
IOWA
does not have a state gem

Iowa does not have a state gem, but there are a few possible candidates, including freshwater pearls and agates. Freshwater pearls have been found in mussels in Iowa's waterways and were especially popular in the late 1800s to early 1900s. Agates are occasionally found as nodules in limestone in various parts of the state and occasionally have very striking bands of color.

MINERAL:
IOWA
does not have a state mineral

Iowa does not have a state mineral, but two good candidates are calcite and quartz. Iowa has a lot of limestone, and calcite crystals often occur in cavities in the limestone. Quartz crystals are typically found in Keokuk geodes, named for the region near the town of Keokuk, where they are found. These geodes can be up to 2 feet across and can contain both quartz and calcite.

A Keokuk geode with quartz and calcite

Side note: The Iowa geode was designated the state stone in 1967.

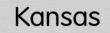

GEM:
JELINITE

(pronounced JEL-lin-ite)
Amber—fossilized resin
Jelinite was designated the state gem in 2018.

Jelinite from Kansas

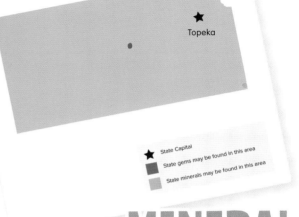

Topeka

★ State Capital

State gems may be found in this area

State minerals may be found in this area

When tree resin gets buried, it can become fossilized into a substance called amber, which is considered to be an organic gemstone. In Kansas there is a rare type of amber called jelinite, named after George Jelinik, a rock collector who found many specimens of it. Jelinite has a yellow-brown color similar to butterscotch and is likely Cretaceous in age, from the time of the dinosaurs. Unfortunately, all the specimens were collected at a location now underwater below Lake Kanopolis.

MINERAL:
GALENA

(pronouced guh-LEEN-uh)
Chemical Formula: **PbS**
Galena was designated the state mineral in 2018

Galena is a metallic mineral that can form crystals with cube or octahedron shapes and is an important source of the element lead, which is used in many industries and valuable for mining. In 1877, rich deposits of galena lead ore were discovered in southeastern Kansas. Within months thousands of people moved there and the mining boomtown of Galena was established. It is part of the Tri-State Mining District along with Missouri and Oklahoma.

Galena from Kansas

le note: Greenhorn limestone was designated the state rock in 2018.

Kentucky

Frankfort

★ State Capital

State gems may be found in this area

State minerals may be found in this area

A pearl from the Tennessee
River region

GEM:
FRESHWATER PEARL

Pearl from Unionida
(pronounced union-I-duh)
order mussels—organic gemstone
The freshwater pearl was designated
the state gem in 1986.

Pearls are organic gemstones, and in Kentucky they're formed by freshwater mussels from the Unionida order. Pearls are formed when something small gets into the mussel and the mussel forms layers of calcium carbonate around the irritant; this results in spheres with shiny, light colors. There are several species of mussels in Lake Kentucky that form pearls, which have been popular as a gemstone in the United States for several decades.

MINERAL:
COAL

(pronounced cole)
Not a mineral; a sedimentary rock
Coal was designated the state mineral in 1998.

A specimen
of coal

Coal is not a mineral because it contains a lot of organic material and is formed as a sedimentary rock. It is formed from vegetation that has been buried and compressed into a carbon-rich rock. For centuries, coal has been used for heating and energy production, and more than 8 billion tons of coal have been mined from Kentucky.

Side note: Kentucky agate was designated the state rock in 2000.

GEM:
CRASSOSTREA VIRGINICA CABOCHON CUT GEMSTONE

The shell of the eastern oyster, Crassostrea virginica

Eastern oystershell

The *Crassostrea virginica* (pronounced crass-o-STREE-uh vir-GIN-eh-kuh) cabochon cut gemstone was designated the state gem in 2011, replacing agate.

Baton Rouge ★

★ State Capital

State gems may be found in this area

State minerals may be found in this area

The eastern oyster is found throughout the eastern US coast and Gulf of Mexico. They have been harvested as food for thousands of years by Native Americans and are more popular than ever today. Large quantities of oystershells are left over after the oysters are eaten by diners, and some of these oystershells can be turned into cabochons (a gem that is polished and rounded rather than cut) and be used in jewelry.

A polished cabochon of eastern oyster, under the trade name LaPearlite®

MINERAL:
AGATE

(pronounced AG-it)

Chemical Formula: SiO_2

Agate was designated the state mineral in 2011 after formerly being the state gem since 1976.

Agate is a variety of chalcedony, which itself is a variety of the mineral quartz. Agate typically has bands or layers of different color, with Louisiana agate in tan, yellow, and reddish colors. In Louisiana, agate is typically found as pebbles and cobbles in the gravel of streams and rivers, and occasionally even in driveway gravel!

An agate from Louisiana

Maine

Augusta

★ State Capital

State gems may be found in this area

State minerals may be found in this area

Fluorapatite from the Pulsifer
Quarry of Maine

GEM:
MAINE
does not have a state gem

Maine does not have a state gem, but one very good candidate is fluorapatite (pronounced floor-AP-i-tite). Found in a few quarries in the state, fluorapatite occurs with a purple color and has a chemical formula of $Ca_5(PO_4)_3F$. One of the sites for the best crystals is Pulsifer Quarry near Auburn, Maine. Many of the crystals from Pulsifer are gem quality, with rich purple colors and good clarity that is worthy of being cut into gemstones.

MINERAL:
TOURMALINE

(pronounced TOUR-ma-leen) | The tourmaline group of minerals
Chemical Formula: most notably Elbaite (pronounced L-bait),
$Na(Li,Al)_3Al_6(BO_3)_3Si_6O_{18}(OH)_4$
Tourmaline was designated the state mineral in 1971.

Watermelon tourmaline from Maine

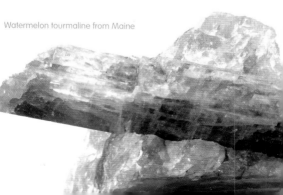

Tourmaline is a group of minerals with similar structures that come in many varieties depending on the elements involved. The minerals can come in almost any color and can have many colors in the same crystal. Elbaite is a colorful tourmaline mineral and includes a variety called "watermelon tourmaline," which features green tourmaline circling a red center. Gem-quality specimens of Elbaite and "watermelon tourmaline" have been found in western Maine since 1820.

GEM:
PATUXENT RIVER STONE

(pronounced puh-TUX-ent)
Chemical Formula: SiO_2
Patuxent River stone was designated the state gem in 2004.

A Patuxent River stone specimen

The Patuxent River stone is a silica stone that is found along the Patuxent River of Maryland. Specimens of the stone can have red and yellow colors, which are present in the Maryland state flag. While it is debated whether the stone is agate (a variety of chalcedony, which is a variety of quartz) or quartzite (metamorphosed quartz sandstone rock), it is agreed that the stone is composed of silica. Some specimens can be nicely polished into cabochons.

Annapolis

★ State Capital
State gems may be found in this area
State minerals may be found in this area

MINERAL:
MARYLAND
does not have a state mineral

Grossular garnet from Rockville, Maryland

Maryland does not have a state mineral but has a variety of minerals that would be good candidates. Gold was mined in parts of the state during the late 1800s to early 1900s. Many types of garnet are also found in stone quarries in the state. Williamsite, a green variety of the mineral antigorite, has been found along the border of the state. The mineral chromite was mined near Baltimore and was important for obtaining the element chromium.

Massachusetts

Boston

★ State Capital

State gems may be found in this area

State minerals may be found in this area

GEM:
RHODONITE

(pronounced ROW-dun-ite)
Chemical Formula: $MnSiO_3$
Rhodonite was designated the state gem in 1979.

Rhodonite from Massachusetts

Rhodonite is a mineral that usually forms in massive pink and red sections and occasionally has blocky crystals. It was found and mined in western Massachusetts in the early 1800s before being abandoned. One location that produced many great specimens was the Betts manganese mine near the town of Plainfield, which mined manganese, an element usually present in rhodonite.

MINERAL:
BABINGTONITE

(pronounced BAB-bing-ton-ite)
Chemical Formula: $Ca_2(Fe,Mn)FeSi_5O_{14}(OH)$
Babingtonite was designated the state mineral in 1981.

Babingtonite from Massachusetts

Babingtonite is an uncommon mineral that forms dark-colored crystals. It contains iron ions, which make it slightly magnetic. In Massachusetts it is found in igneous volcanic rocks, often with other minerals that form in volcanic cavities, such as prehnite and quartz. Since volcanic rocks are mined for industrial purposes, many specimens were found. At one point in the 1940s, ten of the fourteen known occurrences of babingtonite were in Massachusetts.

Side note: Roxbury puddingstone was designated the state rock in 1983.

GEM:
CHLORASTROLITE

(pronounced klor-astro-lite)
Variety of pumpellyite (pronounced pum-PELL-lee-ite)
Chemical Formula: $Ca_2MgAl_2(Si_2O_7)(SiO_4)(OH)_2 \cdot H_2O$
Chlorastrolite was designated the state gem in 1972.

Polished chlorastrolite
from Michigan

Michigan

Lansing

★ State Capital
■ State gems may be found in this area
■ State minerals may be found in this area

Found in the Upper Peninsula of Michigan, chlorastrolite is a variety of the mineral pumpellyite and possesses a greenish color and turtleshell pattern. Chlorastrolite is formed by filling cavities in volcanic basalt. Weathering of the basalt exposed the chlorastrolite, which was then washed by the waves of Lake Superior to form beautiful gem pebbles. A lot of chlorastrolite was found on the shores of Isle Royale before it became a national park in 1940. Collecting it there is now illegal; however, it can still be found in many places in the Upper Peninsula.

Copper crystals from Michigan

MINERAL:
MICHIGAN
does not have a state mineral

Michigan does not have a state mineral, but it should be copper. Copper is found in Michigan's Upper Peninsula, in an area referred to as "Copper Country." The metal has been mined by Native American tribes in the region for thousands of years. The copper boom of the 1800s brought thousands to the state to prospect for copper, and more than 14 billion pounds of copper is believed to have been mined in the state.

e note: Petoskey stone was declared the state stone in 1965.

Minnesota

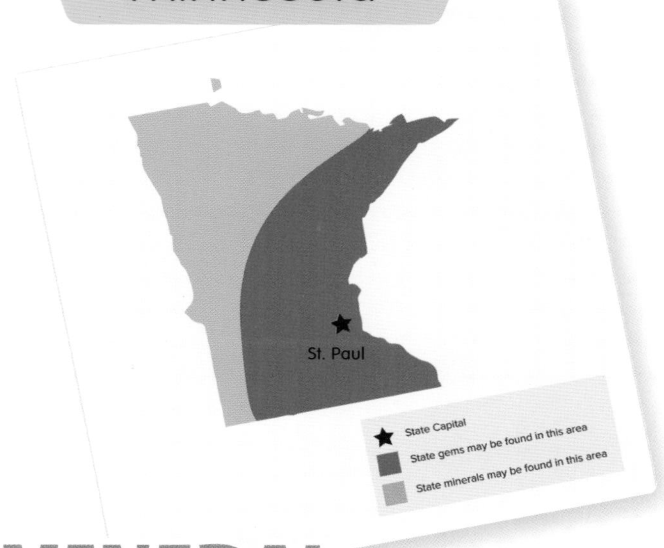

State Capital
★ St. Paul

★ State Capital

State gems may be found in this area

State minerals may be found in this area

GEM:
LAKE SUPERIOR AGATE

(pronounced AG-it)
Chemical Formula: SiO_2
Lake Superior agate was designated the state gem in 1969.

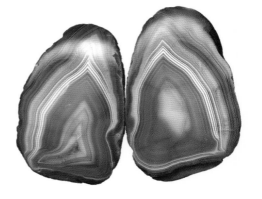

Lake Superior agate from Minnesota

MINERAL:

MINNESOTA
does not have a state mineral

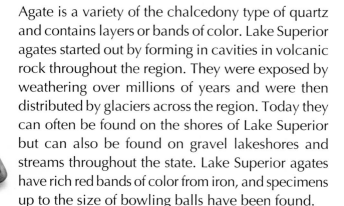

Hematite iron ore from Minnesota

Agate is a variety of the chalcedony type of quartz and contains layers or bands of color. Lake Superior agates started out by forming in cavities in volcanic rock throughout the region. They were exposed by weathering over millions of years and were then distributed by glaciers across the region. Today they can often be found on the shores of Lake Superior but can also be found on gravel lakeshores and streams throughout the state. Lake Superior agates have rich red bands of color from iron, and specimens up to the size of bowling balls have been found.

Minnesota does not have a state mineral; however, the state produces the most iron ore in the country. The Mesabi Iron Range in the northeast section of the state is a large deposit of iron ore. The iron was deposited during the middle Precambrian, about 1.8 billion years ago, when the erosion of mountains released iron into seawater and an oxidation event caused iron to settle out of the water and form layers. Iron is also mined in a rock called taconite, which is composed of iron minerals interlayered with other minerals. Hematite is one of the primary iron ore minerals from the region.

GEM:
MISSISSIPPI
does not have
a state gem

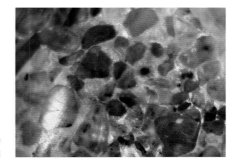

A close-up of
Mississippi opal

Mississippi does not have a state gem, but a recent discovery of precious opal has potential. In many other places, opal is found in volcanic rhyolite or sedimentary limestone, but in Mississippi the opal is found as part of quartzite in the Catahoula formation. The opal helps hold together the sand and quartz particles. The material can be polished into cabochons that sparkle with color. Currently only a small amount of the material has been found, but it is hoped that more will be found in the future.

Mississippi opal polished into a
cabochon

Jackson

★ State Capital

State gems may be found in this area

State minerals may be found in this area

MINERAL:
MISSISSIPPI
does not have a state mineral

Selenite from
Mississippi

Mississippi does not have a state mineral, but one very good candidate is selenite (pronounced SELL-en-ite). While selenite is a variety of the mineral gypsum and has the same chemical makeup ($CaSO_4 \cdot 2H_2O$), it is the name typically used for crystals of gypsum. In Mississippi it can be found in clay deposits, with many great clear crystals being found in Yazoo clay. Selenite is very soft—a 2 on the Mohs scale—and can be scratched by fingernails.

enote: Petrified wood was designated the state rock in 1976.

Missouri

Jefferson City

★ State Capital

State gems may be found in this area

State minerals may be found in this area

Agates from near St. Louis, Missouri

GEM:
MISSOURI
does not have a state gem

Calcite from Missouri

Missouri does not have a state gem, but it has some interesting minerals that could potentially be turned into gemstones. The leading candidate is calcite, which is often found as yellow and orange crystals associated with metallic minerals from mining in the western portions of the state. Another potential state gem is fluorite, which is found in the eastern side of the state. While both minerals are considered soft (3 to 4 on the Mohs scale), they can be cut into faceted gemstones with great clarity and nice colors. Agate is also found in a few places in the state and might make for a good candidate.

MINERAL:
GALENA

(pronounced guh-LEEN-uh)
Chemical Formula: **PbS**
Galena was designated the state mineral in 1967.

Galena is a mineral that contains high percentages of the element lead, an important economic metal; pure galena is 86 percent lead. It forms dark metallic crystals in cubic and octahedral crystals. Large quantities of galena lead ore were found in Missouri, making it at one point in time the world's highest producer of lead. More than 17 million tons of lead has been mined in the state since the 1700s. Missouri is part of the Tri-State Mining District with Kansas and Oklahoma.

Galena from Missouri

Sidenote: Mozarkite was designated the state rock in 1967.

GEM:
SAPPHIRE AND MONTANA AGATE

(pronounced SA-fire)

Chemical Formula: Al_2O_3 and SiO_2

The sapphire and Montana agate were designated the state gems in 1969.

Yogo sapphires from Montana

Moss agate from Montana

Montana designated two gems at the same time. Sapphires were found in Montana in the late 1800s and initially were not considered valuable, since prospectors were looking for gold. Eventually, sapphires from Montana were recognized as one of America's great gemstones, with special focus on the cornflower-blue Yogo sapphires from Yogo Gulch.

Montana agate is popularly found along the Yellowstone River but can be found in gravel banks throughout the eastern portion of the state. It comes in many colors, including white, tans, and yellows, but one of the prettiest types is "moss agate," which contains mineralized dendritic patterns that look like plants.

Helena

★ State Capital

◼ Sapphires may be found in this area

◼ Agate may be found in this area

MINERAL:
MONTANA
does not have a state mineral

Pyrite in chalcocite from Butte, Montana

Montana does not have a state mineral, but the state's rich mineral landscape provides many for consideration. In the town of Butte is the Berkeley Pit, which is a 1-mile-long and 1,780-foot-deep water-filled pit that is the remnants of a copper mine that also produced gold and silver. Other metallic minerals such as pyrite were also found there. Rhodochrosite has also been found around Butte. In southern Montana is the Stillwater Complex, an important large body of chromium ore that also has interesting rare platinum and palladium minerals.

38

Nebraska

Lincoln ★

★ State Capital
State gems may be found in this area
State minerals may be found in this area

GEM:
CHALCEDONY / BLUE AGATE

(pronounced cal-SED-nee)
A variety of quartz
Chemical Formula: SiO_2

Chalcedony stone, blue agate, was designated the state gem in 1967.

Blue agate from Nebraska

Blue agate is a variety of the chalcedony type of quartz, and specimens from Nebraska have a beautiful range of sky-blue colors with bands of white. The chalcedony formed when silica-rich water flowed into faults and fractures in bedrock and deposited it, likely colored by trace elements such as iron.

MINERAL:
NEBRASKA
does not have a state mineral

Sidenote: Prairie agate was designated the state rock in 1967.

Nebraska does not have a state mineral, and, while agate chalcedony is very popular, there are a few other interesting minerals. Celestine (also called celestite) is a strontium mineral with a light-blue color that has been found in a few small deposits in the state. Nebraska also has some rare quartz pseudomorphs of gypsum. A pseudomorph is when one mineral replaces another but keeps the original mineral's form; in this case, gypsum crystal clusters have been replaced by quartz.

Celestine or celestite from Nebraska

PRECIOUS GEM:
VIRGIN VALLEY BLACK FIRE OPAL

(pronounced O-puhl)
Chemical Formula: $SiO_2 \cdot nH_2O$
Virgin Valley black fire opal was designated the state precious gem in 1987.

Opal from Virgin Valley, Nevada

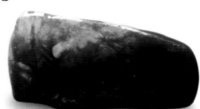

Fire opal gemstone from Virgin Valley, Nevada

Carson City

★ State Capital

State precious gems may be found in this area

State semi-precious gems may be found in this area

A small area of northern Nevada called Virgin Valley is responsible for the finest opals from the United States. About twelve to fifteen million years ago, volcanic ash and tuff buried many trees in the area. Silica-rich water replaced many of these buried trees with opal. The opal of Virgin Valley comes in many colors, ranging from clear and milky to black with brilliant flashes of red, green, and blue color (which is where it gets its name). There are several mining claims in the valley that have operated for nearly a century, and many of them welcome visitors to pay to dig.

SEMIPRECIOUS GEM:
NEVADA TURQUOISE

(pronounced ter-coiz)
Chemical Formula: $CuAl_6(PO_4)_4(OH)_8 \cdot 4H_2O$
Nevada turquoise was designated the state semiprecious gem in 1987.

Turquoise is a secondary mineral that usually forms near copper or other minerals. It's traditionally considered to be a "semiprecious" gemstone, but it can be quite valuable. In Nevada there are numerous claims producing turquoise, and it is found throughout the state in various shades of blue.

Nevada *continued*

Royston turquoise from Nevada

Topaz crystal
from Nevada

Earrings featuring Royston ribbon
turquoise from Nevada

Side note: Silver was designated the state metal in 1977.
Sandstone was designated the state rock in 1987.

MINERAL:

NEVADA
does not have a state mineral

Nevada does not have a state mineral but is a mineral-rich state. Gold has been found in many parts of Nevada, and quartz is present in numerous varieties. Other notable minerals include various garnets, calcite, barite, sulfur, and others. The Zapot pegmatite in the Gillis Range has produced great topaz crystals that fluoresce under ultraviolet light.

Gold from Nevada

GEM:
SMOKY QUARTZ

(pronounced ka-wort-s)
Chemical Formula: SiO_2
Smoky quartz was designated the state gem in 1985.

Smoky quartz from New Hampshire

New Hampshire has a lot of the rock granite, and smoky quartz is often one of the components of granite. Smoky quartz is quartz with dark coloring, which it gets from silicon that has been freed by irradiation. Smoky quartz can be seen as dark crystalline forms in granite but can also form nice crystals in pockets and is found throughout most of the state.

New Hampshire

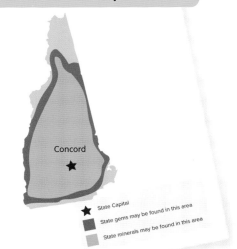

Concord

★ State Capital
State gems may be found in this area
State minerals may be found in this area

MINERAL:
BERYL

(pronounced BEHR-uhl)
Chemical Formula: $Be_3Al_2(Si_6O_{18})$
Beryl was designated the state mineral in 1985.

Beryl is a mineral that forms several varieties of gemstones depending on its color, including aquamarine, emerald, heliodor, and others. Beryl can also be found in granite, especially granitic pegmatites, of which there are several in New Hampshire. While most of New Hampshire's beryls are white or pale colored, occasionally good-quality light-blue aquamarines have been found.

Beryl from New Hampshire

Granite was designated the state rock in 1985.

de note:

New Jersey

Trenton

★ State Capital

State gems may be found in this area

State minerals may be found in this area

Rough amber from New Jersey

GEM:
NEW JERSEY
does not have a state gem

New Jersey does not have a state gem but has several great candidates. Corundum (pronounced coe-RUN-dum), with the occasional ruby variety, is found in several quarries in the mineral-rich northwestern part of the state. Prehnite is a green mineral found in volcanic rocks in the north of the state and is among the best-quality prehnite in the world. One very notable potential gemstone is amber from near Sayreville. Cretaceous-age amber has been collected for decades in lignites and clays near Sayreville and can contain rare fossils that provide a glimpse into the Cretaceous.

A slice of amber from New Jersey

MINERAL:
NEW JERSEY
does not have a state mineral

New Jersey does not have a state mineral, but it really should be the combination of franklinite-willemite-calcite from the Franklin ore body, a 1.3 billion-year-old marble in northern New Jersey. It is rich in the element zinc and has more than 350 different minerals. More than ninety of these minerals are fluorescent under ultraviolet lights, including the mineral willemite, which fluoresces a bright green, and calcite, which fluoresces red. Franklinite is a nonfluorescent zinc mineral usually found with willemite and calcite. Together, the combination of minerals creates festive colors under ultraviolet lights.

A sphere from the Franklin ore body, under normal light, and fluorescing under UV light

GEM:
TURQUOISE

(pronounced ter-coiz)
Chemical Formula:
$$CuAl_6(PO_4)_4(OH)_8 \cdot 4H_2O$$
Turquoise was designated the
state gem in 1967.

Turquoise has been mined in New Mexico for at least a thousand years by Native American cultures, as evidenced by ancient mining sites and turquoise artifacts found at archeological sites throughout the American Southwest. Turquoise is usually found near weathering copper deposits and comes in shades of blue colors. Today turquoise is still mined in the state and used in Native American jewelry, including the Squash Blossom Necklace, which is the official necklace of New Mexico.

New Mexico

Santa Fe

★ State Capital
State gems may be found in this area
State minerals may be found in this area

Turquoise cabochon from the
Tyrone Mine of New Mexico

MINERAL:
NEW MEXICO
does not have a state mineral

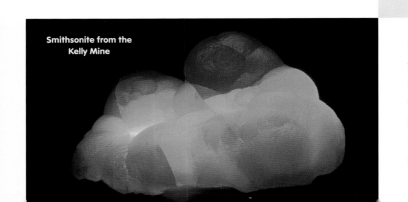

Smithsonite from the
Kelly Mine

New Mexico does not have a state mineral, but one prominent mineral that is found there is smithsonite (pronounced SMITH-son-night). The mineral is named after English chemist and mineralogist James Smithson, who first discovered it was a separate mineral from another zinc mineral and who left money to establish the Smithsonian Institution in Washington, DC. In New Mexico, some of the world's best smithsonite has been found at the Kelly Mine, with blue colors and round botryoidal crystals.

New York

Albany

State Capital

State gems may be found in this area

State minerals may be found in this area

Charles R. Barton Jr. looking at a wall of garnets at Gore Mountain, 1961

Faceted garnet from Gore Mountain, New York

MINERAL:

NEW YORK
does not have a state mineral

GEM:
GARNET

(pronounced GAR-net)
The garnet group of minerals
Chemical Formula:
$(Ca,Mg,Fe_2+, Mn2+)_3(Al,Fe_3+,Mn_3+, V_3+,Cr_3+)_2(SiO_4)_3$
Garnet was designated the state gem in 1969.

Garnets are a group of minerals with similar structures that form crystals that can be cut into gemstones. Garnets also tend to be hard, so they are mined to be turned into abrasives. Gore Mountain, in upstate New York, is one of the world's largest garnet deposits and was mined by the Barton Mines Corporation for more than a century. Most of the almandine garnets found there are baseball sized, and garnets up to 3 feet across have been found! The old mine site now has tours, and visitors can hunt for their own deep-red almandine garnets.

New York does not have a state mineral, but it has a famous type of quartz called the Herkimer diamond. Found in pockets in outcrops of dolomite in Herkimer County, Herkimer diamonds are double-terminated crystals of quartz with great clarity and crystal structure. Several mines in the area allow paying visitors to try to mine crystals. There have been attempts before to get Herkimer diamonds designated as the state mineral, but they have not yet been successful.

Herkimer diamond quartz crystals

PRECIOUS GEM:
EMERALD

(pronounced EM-er-ruld)
Variety of beryl
Chemical Formula: $Be_3Al_2(Si_6O_{18})$
Emerald was designated the state precious stone in 1973.

While technically designated as a precious stone, emerald is a gem variety of the mineral beryl, with various green colors due to traces of the elements chromium and vanadium. In the United States, gem-quality emerald has been found only in North Carolina. Emerald crystals up to 7.5 inches long have been found in pockets in Alexander County.

Emerald crystals from North Carolina

Raleigh

★ State Capital

State gems may be found in this area

State minerals may be found in this area

MINERAL:
GOLD

(pronounced gohld)
Chemical Formula: Au
Gold was designated the state mineral in 2011.

Gold from North Carolina

North Carolina was the site of America's first gold rush after a 17-pound gold nugget was discovered by a teenager in a creek in 1799. For the next several decades, North Carolina was the leader in gold production in the United States. Many gold mines were set up in North Carolina's gold belt, and they reached up to 800 feet deep. Many former mines are now tourist destinations where visitors can try their hand at gold panning.

de note: Granite was designated the state rock in 1979.

North Dakota

Bismarck

★ State Capital

■ State gems may be found in this area

■ State minerals may be found in this area

Agates from North Dakota

GEM:
NORTH DAKOTA
does not have a state gem

North Dakota does not have a state gem. Much of the state is covered by material brought down from farther north by glaciers. In the glacial material, some agate chalcedony can be found, often already in a semipolished form. Most often they come in yellow and orange colors. Small amounts of amber have also been found in the state in Cretaceous deposits.

MINERAL:
NORTH DAKOTA
does not have a state mineral

North Dakota does not have a state mineral, but a candidate is the clear crystal form of gypsum called selenite, which can be found weathering out of clay in many parts of the state. These often form nice clear crystal masses. Quartz in the form of agate chalcedony can be found in glacial deposits throughout the state.

Selenite crystal from North Dakota

GEM:
OHIO FLINT

(pronounced FLINT)
Chemical Formula: SiO_2
Ohio flint was designated the state gem in 1965.

Polished Ohio flint

Flint is a hard variety of the sedimentary rock chert and has been used by Native Americans for thousands of years. When struck at particular angles, flint will produce a sharp edge that is perfect for knives and arrowheads. Ohio flint comes in a variety of colors, including mixes of red, orange, tan, gray, and white. These colors and the ability to take a nice polish make it perfect for turning into polished gemstones.

Ohio

Columbus

★ State Capital

State gems may be found in this area

State minerals may be found in this area

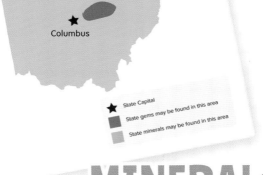

Celestine from Clay
Center, Ohio

MINERAL:

OHIO
does not have a state mineral

Ohio does not have a state mineral but has many candidates. The Findlay Arch Mining District of northwestern Ohio has numerous quarries mining dolomite, and they come across many minerals during the process. Yellow calcite crystals are found in veins and pockets along with fluorite crystals. Celestine or celestite—a mineral with blue and white crystals—is also often found with the previous two minerals. There is even a giant geode with celestine crystals up to 3 feet wide, called Crystal Cave, that people can visit in Put-in-Bay, Ohio.

Fluorite from Ohio

Oklahoma

★ Oklahoma City

★ State Capital
State gems may be found in this area
State minerals may be found in this area

GEM:
OKLAHOMA
does not have a state gem

Ruby Jack sphalerite from Picher, Oklahoma

MINERAL:
OKLAHOMA
does not have a state mineral

Oklahoma does not have a state gem, but one possibility is sphalerite (pronounced SFAL-ler-rite). A zinc sulfide mineral with a chemical formula of $(Zn,Fe)S$, sphalerite is often found while miners are searching for lead. Sphalerite usually forms dark opaque crystals that look metallic. On rare occasions, a type of sphalerite called Ruby Jack can be found, which is translucent and has a dark-red color. Ruby Jack sphalerite has been found in Oklahoma in the northeastern Tri-State Mining District.

Oklahoma does not have a state mineral, but there are many minerals in the Tri-State Mining District in the northeastern portion of the state. The Tri-State district runs through Oklahoma, Kansas, and Missouri and contains large amounts of metallic ores mined for lead and zinc. Galena is one of the primary minerals for lead ore and comes in interesting crystal varieties, such as cubes and octahedrons. Calcite is often found during lead ore mining. Sphalerite was primarily mined for zinc ore. The mineral dolomite is also found in many places in the state.

Galena from Picher, Oklahoma

Side note: Barite rose was designated the state rock in 1968. Hourglass selenite was designated the state crystal in 2005.

GEM:
OREGON SUNSTONE

Labradorite (pronounced LAB-bruh-dor-rite)
Chemical Formula:
$(Ca,Na)[Al(Al,Si)Si_2O_8]$
Oregon sunstone was designated the state gem in 1987.

Faceted Oregon sunstone

Oregon sunstone is a gem variety of the mineral labradorite from the feldspar group. It has microscopic inclusions of copper, making it unique among sunstones, and these inclusions give it a property called aventurescence, where light glitters off the tiny inclusions. Usually, Oregon sunstone is found in colors of orange and red but can also be found colorless, or even green. It is mined at several sites out of volcanic rock.

Nugget of josephinite

State Capital
State gems may be found in this area
State minerals may be found in this area

MINERAL:
OREGONITE & JOSEPHINITE

(pronounced OR-reh-gun-nite and Joe-seh-fien-ite)
Chemical Formula: Ni_2Fe and (awaurite) Ni_3Fe | Oregonite and josephinite were designated as the official twin state minerals in 2013.

Oregonite specimen

Oregonite and josephinite are both found as nuggets in Josephine Creek in Oregon and have a similar appearance, which is why they're designated as the twin state minerals of Oregon. Josephinite is the local name for the mineral awaurite. Both oregonite and josephinite contain nickel iron alloys that are rare on Earth and are similar to that of the makeup of meteorites, which makes the minerals very interesting for geologists to study.

de note: The thunderegg was designated the state rock in 1965.

Pennsylvania

Harrisburg

★ State Capital

State gems may be found in this area

State minerals may be found in this area

Amethyst from
Pennsylvania

Faceted amethyst
gemstone

PENNSYLVANIA
does not have a state gem

MINERAL:
PENNSYLVANIA
does not have a state mineral

Pennsylvania does not have a state mineral, but a top contender is celestine, which is one of a handful of minerals that were first discovered in Pennsylvania. It's a strontium sulfate mineral and often has white- to blue-colored crystals with varying clarity. Celestine has been proposed as the state mineral in multiple legislative bills over the years, but none have been passed. Quartz, which is found in many places in the state, has also been proposed as the state mineral.

Pennsylvania does not have a state gem, but there are a few possibilities. Amethyst (pronounced AM-meh-thist) is the purple variety of quartz, and some specimens have been found in the southeastern portion of the state. Amethyst adorns the crown of the winner of Miss Pennsylvania every year, although the gems are mostly from Brazil. Recently, a bill to designate amethyst as the state gem was brought to the legislature.

Celestine from
Pennsylvania

GEM:
RHODE ISLAND
does not have a state gem

Danalite from Rhode Island

Rhode Island does not have a state gem. Smoky quartz and amethyst have been found in a few quarries in the state and are good candidates. Another candidate is danalite, a mineral named after famed American mineralogist James Dwight Dana, which has a chemical formula of $Fe_4Be_3(SiO_4)_3S$. Specimens of danalite have been found in Rhode Island and contain a nice light-pink color that may be worthy of being polished into a gem.

Amethyst from Rhode Island

Providence

State Capital
State gems may be found in this area
State minerals may be found in this area

MINERAL:
BOWENITE

(pronounced BOE-wen-nite) Variety of antigorite
Chemical Formula: $Mg_3(Si_2O_5)(OH)_4$
Bowenite was designated the state mineral in 1966.

While it was first scientifically described and named in 1850 from specimens from Rhode Island, bowenite has been used by the Maori culture of New Zealand for hundreds of years to make tools and weapons. Bowenite is a variety of the mineral antigorite and usually has a light-to-dark-green color. While it can be gem quality from localities in other countries, the specimens from Rhode Island tend to be opaque.

Bowenite from Rhode Island

e note:

Cumberlandite was designated the state rock in 1966.

South Carolina

State Capital ★
State gems may be found in this area
State minerals may be found in this area

Columbia ★

Amethyst from
South Carolina

GEM:
AMETHYST

(pronounced AM-meh-thist)
Variety of quartz
Chemical Formula: SiO_2
Amethyst was designated the state gem in 1969.

Amethyst is a variety of the mineral quartz. It is distinguished from other varieties of quartz by its purple color, which is often from irradiation or from elemental impurities. In South Carolina, amethyst has been found at several mines throughout the state, including at least one mine that welcomes visitors. South Carolina amethyst comes in various shades of purple and can often be double terminated, where the crystal has a point at each end instead of just one.

MINERAL:
SOUTH CAROLINA
does not have a state mineral

South Carolina does not have a state mineral but has a few potential candidate minerals. Gold was mined in several areas in the state in the 1800s and is still being found today. Beryl is also found in the state, including the blue aquamarine variety. The mineral zircon (pronounced zir-con) has also been found with a purple color and octahedral crystals. While zircon can be found in many states, the specimens from South Carolina are larger and better formed.

Zircon crystal from
South Carolina

 Side note: Blue granite was designated the state stone in 1969.

GEM:
FAIRBURN AGATES

(pronounced AG-its)
Variety of the chalcedony type
of quartz
Chemical Formula: SiO_2
Fairburn agates were designated
the state gem in 1966.

Named after a small town near where they are often found, Fairburn agates are beautiful nodules with fortification banding. Fortification banding is a property where the color bands of the agate are parallel and turn at sharp angles. The colors of Fairburn agates include bright reds, whites, and blues. Typically, Fairburn agates are smaller than a golf ball, and larger ones with good banded colors are exceptionally rare.

Fairburn agate from
South Dakota

Fairburn agate from
South Dakota

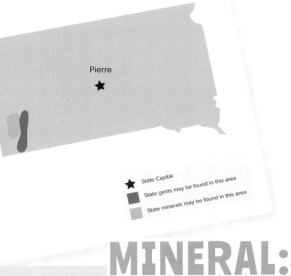

Pierre

★ State Capital

State gems may be found in this area

State minerals may be found in this area

MINERAL:
ROSE QUARTZ

(pronounced ka-wort-s)
Variety of quartz
Chemical Formula: SiO_2
Rose quartz was designated the state gem in 1966.

Rose quartz is a variety of the mineral quartz and was named for its pink color. Rose quartz rarely forms crystals and is usually found in large blocks and veins, making it good for carving, polishing, and tumbling. Rose quartz tends to have an internal cloudy look caused by microscopic mineral fibers.

Rose quartz from
South Dakota

Tennessee

Necklace with
Tennessee pearl

Nashville

★ State Capital

State gems may be found in this area

State minerals may be found in this area

A Tennessee pearl

GEM:
TENNESSEE PEARL

(pronounced piryl)
Pearl from the Unionida (pronounced union-I-da) order of freshwater
mussels—organic gemstone
The Tennessee pearl was designated
the state gem in 1979.

Pearls are hard organic gemstones formed by some molluscs, and have been used as jewelry for thousands of years. In Tennessee, freshwater mussels from the Unionida order occasionally form pearls and have been found in the Tennessee River, Kentucky Lake, and a few other bodies of water. When a particle of debris gets into a mussel, they form layers of calcium carbonate around it, which results in a pearl with shiny light colors. After freshwater-pearl-forming mussels were discovered in Tennessee, many pearl farms were established to grow and harvest pearls, but only one still exists today.

MINERAL:
AGATE

(pronounced AG-it)
Variety of the chalcedony type of quartz
Chemical Formula: SiO_2 | Agate was designated the state stone in 1969 and redesignated the state mineral in 2009.

Paint Rock agate from
Tennessee

Tennessee has a few deposits of high-quality colorful agates with great hues of color in red and orange. One of the more popular agates from Tennessee are "Paint Rock agates," which can have rich bands of bright color. Today most Paint Rock agates are found as nodules embedded in limestone, but occasionally they can be found loose in gravel beds.

Side note: Limestone was designated the state rock in 1979.

GEM:
TEXAS BLUE TOPAZ

(pronounced TOE-paz)
Chemical Formula: $Al_2SiO_4(F,OH)_2$
Texas blue topaz was designated the state gem in 1969.

Blue topaz crystal
from Texas

Austin

★ State Capital
State gems may be found in this area
State minerals may be found in this area

Faceted topaz from Texas
with the Lone Star cut

Topaz is a fairly hard mineral—8 on the Mohs scale—and tends to form crystals with good clarity, which makes it popular as a gemstone. In Texas, topaz is found near areas of granite, with the best-known location being Mason County, where rare blue topaz has been found. A crystal believed to be the largest gem-quality topaz crystal from the United States, weighing 2.85 pounds, was found in Mason County. A few ranches allow people to try to hunt for their own topaz for a fee.

Side note: Silver was designated the state precious metal in 2007. Palmwood was designated the state stone in 1969. Texas also has an official state gemstone cut, the "Lone Star cut," which was designated in 1977 and features a star cut into a gemstone—usually a topaz.

MINERAL:
TEXAS
does not have a state mineral

Bouquet agate from Texas

Texas does not have a state mineral, but there are several good mineral candidates. Pyrite (pronounced PIE-rite) is often found in limestone deposits in parts of the state. Selenite crystals can be found in clay deposits. Of note is a variety of agate quartz found in the West Texas region, including rare fire agate, which have shimmering ranges of colors.

Utah

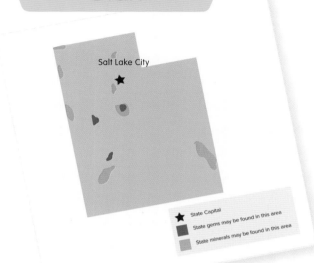

Salt Lake City ★

★ State Capital

State gems may be found in this area

State minerals may be found in this area

Topaz crystal from Utah

GEM:
TOPAZ

(pronounced TOE-paz)
Chemical Formula: $Al_2SiO_4(F,OH)_2$
Topaz was designated the state gem in 1969.

Topaz is a hard mineral that forms nice crystals, often with good clarity, that are suitable for cutting into gemstones. In Utah, topaz is usually found in pockets in volcanic rhyolite and is often found throughout the Thomas Range Mountains. The crystals are typically fingernail sized with great clarity and a tan color. There are several well-known collecting sites and a pay-to-dig site for Utah topaz.

MINERAL:
COPPER

(pronounced CAH-per)
Chemical Formula: Cu
Copper was designated the state mineral in 1994.

Copper is an element used in many industries and can be found in the Bingham Canyon Open Pit Copper Mine near Salt Lake City. It is the deepest open-pit mine in the world, at a depth of 3,900 feet and measuring 2.5 miles wide. The mine has produced more than 20 million tons of copper in its lifetime. Copper and copper ore are also associated with many colorful minerals such as azurite and turquoise that are found in many areas of Utah.

Copper crystal from Utah

Side note: Coal was designated the state rock in 1991.

Montpelier

★ State Capital
■ State gems may be found in this area
■ State minerals may be found in this area

GEM:
GROSSULAR GARNET

(pronounced GRAUS-yoo-ler GAR-net)
Chemical Formula: $Ca_3Al_2(SiO_4)_3$
Grossular garnet was designated the state gem in 1992.

Grossular garnet from Eden Mills, Vermont

Grossular garnets are a variety of garnet that contains calcium and aluminum. While they can have green and red colors, the grossular garnets from quarries near the town of Eden Mills, Vermont, have famously had a light-orange color with great clarity. The quarries were mining industrial minerals, and the garnets were a pleasant surprise.

Talc from Vermont

MINERAL:
TALC

(pronounced taellk)
Chemical Formula: $Mg_3Si_4O_{10}(OH)_2$
Talc was designated the state mineral in 1992.

Considered to be the softest mineral, talc is a 1 on the Mohs scale of hardness and can be scratched with just your fingernail. Talc is mined and used for many things, including baby powder, cosmetics, and various other products. Vermont has a lot of metamorphic rock that contain large quantities of talc, making the state one of the top talc producers in the country.

Sidenote: Vermont designated three state rocks in 1992: granite, marble, and slate.

Virginia

Richmond

★ State Capital
State gems may be found in this area
State minerals may be found in this area

GEM:
VIRGINIA
does not have a state mineral

Amazonite from Virginia

Virginia does not have a state gem, but amazonite is one of the best candidates. Amazonite (pronounced AM-muh-zon-nite) is a variety of the mineral microcline and is distinguished by its bright-greenish colors, which range from apple green to teal. The Morefield Gem Mine near the town of Amelia is the best source of amazonite in the eastern United States. The mine digs into a pegmatite deposit and has crystalline masses of amazonite up to several feet across.

MINERAL:
VIRGINIA
does not have a state mineral

Virginia does not have a state mineral, but there are a variety of interesting minerals in various parts of the state. Near the city of Fairfax, some interesting zeolite group minerals such as apophyllite (pronounced uh-POFF-fil-lite) and prehnite (pronounced PRE-en-nite) have been found, often with good color and nice crystal structures. Rhodonite is also found in the state, and there have been attempts to commercially mine it for gems. Quartz, staurolite, kyanite, and other minerals are found in the state as well.

Rhodonite from Virginia

Side note:

Nelsonite was designated the state rock in 2016.

Apophyllite on prehnite from Virginia

GEM:
PETRIFIED WOOD

Fossilized wood replaced by minerals. Petrified wood was designated the state gem in 1975.

Petrified wood from Washington

Petrified wood is created through a process called permineralization. Essentially, a tree dies and gets buried by sediment, and then all its internal cells are replaced by minerals to become petrified. Most often, quartz is the mineral that replaces trees and has different colors due to trace elements. In Washington State, petrified wood can be found in many areas, and some of it is beautiful enough to be polished into gemstones. Ginkgo Petrified Forest State Park, near Kittitas, was established in 1935 to preserve a variety of petrified wood from about fifteen million years ago, with dozens of species having been found there.

Amethyst from Washington

Washington

Olympia

★ State Capital

State gems may be found in this area

State minerals may be found in this area

MINERAL:
WASHINGTON
does not have a state mineral

Washington does not have a state mineral, but there are many interesting minerals throughout the Cascade Range Mountains in the state. Vesper Peak is a locality that has produced many great specimens of grossular garnets over the past few decades, often with gemmy orange-brown crystals. Amethyst has also been found in a few locations in the Cascades, often with great color and nice, small clusters of crystals. Spruce Ridge is a location with nice quartz crystals growing with pyrite crystals.

Grossular garnets from Vesper Peak

West Virginia

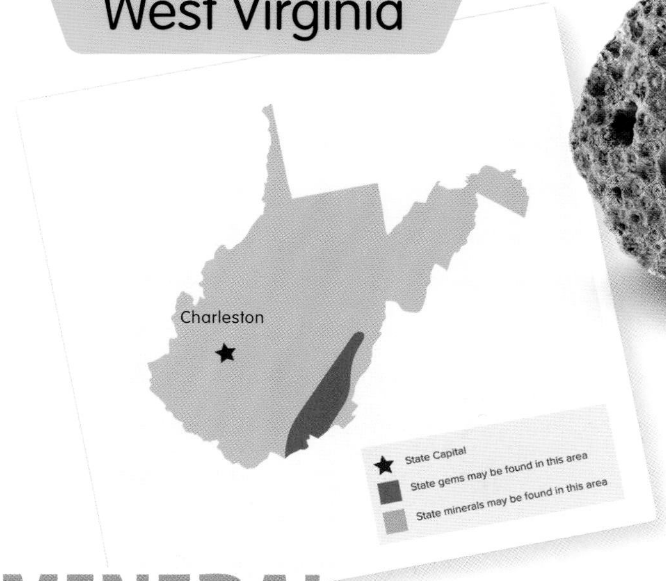

Charleston ★

★ State Capital

State gems may be found in this area

State minerals may be found in this area

Rough *Lithostrotionella* fossil coral from West Virginia

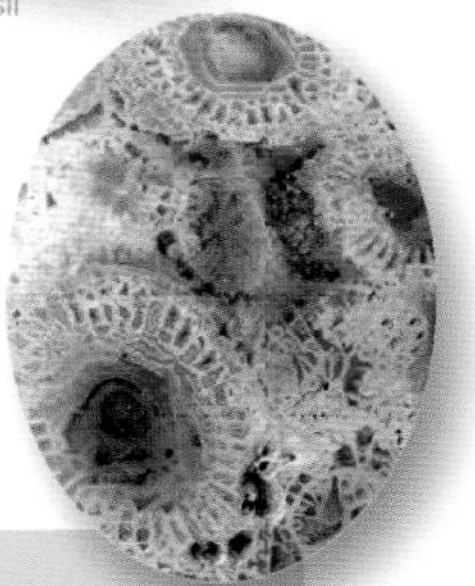

Polished *Lithostro-tionella* fossil coral from West Virginia

GEM:
LITHOSTROTION-ELLA, WEST VIRGINIA CORAL CHALCEDONY

(pronounced LITH-o-stroe-shun-NELL-uh) Silicified fossil coral of the *Lithostrotionella* genus. *Lithostrotionella*, West Virginia coral chalcedony, was designated the state gem in 1990.

Corals are colonies built by individual organisms known as polyps. They consist of calcium carbonate and have been around for hundreds of millions of years. In West Virginia there are fossilized corals of the *Lithostrotionella* genus, where the coral structure has been infilled and replaced with silica to form the chalcedony type of quartz. The *Lithostrontionella* are from the Mississippian subperiod of geologic time, which was about 358 to 323 million years ago. The silica preservation allows them to be polished into cabochons.

MINERAL:

WEST VIRGINIA
does not have a state mineral

West Virginia does not have a state mineral, but there are a few good candidates. Calcite is found in many places throughout the state, often as small yellow crystals in cavities in rocks. Selenite, the clear crystal variety of gypsum, is found in many of the clay deposits in the state. Other common minerals include pyrite and varieties of quartz.

Selenite crystal from West Virginia

Sidenote: Bituminous coal was designated the state rock in 2009.

GEM:
WISCONSIN
does not have a state gem

Moonstone from
Wisconsin

Madison ★

★ State Capital

State gems may be found in this area

State minerals may be found in this area

Wisconsin does not have a state gem, but two good candidates include moonstone and Lake Superior agate. Moonstone is a variety of the mineral feldspar and has a shimmering effect when viewed at certain angles. Specimens can be found in the Stettin area of central Wisconsin, where there are granite outcrops. They have the potential to be polished into cabochon gems. Lake Superior agate can be found in gravel in St. Croix County, and, like the Lake Superior type of agates of many states, it was likely transported there by glaciers.

Lake Superior agate from
Wisconsin

MINERAL:
GALENA
(pronounced guh-LEEN-uh)
Chemical Formula: **PbS**
Galena was designated the state mineral in 1971.

Galena is one of the main types of lead ore because it contains high amounts of lead, which is used in many industries. For hundreds of years, Native Americans have mined the lead ore in the region that is now southwestern Wisconsin. In the early 1800s, thousands of miners moved to that region to dig for lead ore, which was found to be surprisingly shallow and easy to reach.

de note: Red granite was designated the state rock in 1971.

Galena from
Wisconsin

Wyoming

Cheyenne

★ State Capital

State gems may be found in this area

State minerals may be found in this area

Nephrite jade from Wyoming

GEM:
JADE

(pronounced Jae-d)
Nephrite
Chemical Formula:
$Ca_2(Mg,Fe)_5Si_8O_{22}(OH)_2$
Jade was designated the state
gemstone in 1967.

There are many stories about when nephrite jade was first discovered in Wyoming, but the value of jade was not appreciated until the Wyoming jade rush of the late 1930s. Jade was found throughout central Wyoming as cobbles and boulders during the 1930s and 1940s, as many people rushed to the region to try to make their fortune. Wyoming jade is the mineral nephrite (the other form of jade is the mineral jadeite), and specimens from Wyoming have green colors ranging from apple green to emerald.

MINERAL:
WYOMING
does not have a state mineral

Wyoming does not have a state mineral, but the state has the world's largest deposit of the mineral trona (pronounced TROE-nuh). An evaporite mineral, trona is mined and processed into baking soda, and Wyoming produces 90 percent of the United States' supply. The mineral is found in the Green River formation and was formed about fifty million years ago, when giant lakes covered parts of the states of Wyoming, Utah, and Colorado. Wyoming mines several million tons of trona a year.

Trona from Wyoming

GLOSSARY

amber: Fossilized tree resin

anhedral: A crystalline mass with no crystal faces

anion: A negatively charged ion or atom

asterism: Property of some gemstones where a star shape is visible at certain angles

atoms: The building blocks of all matter. Identified as elements.

aventurescence: Metallic shimmering effect of minerals and gems

cabochon: A round, polished gemstone

carbon: A chemical element that is an important component of life

cavity: A hole in a rock or other object

chalcedony: A type of quartz that has microscopic crystal masses, giving an overall smooth appearance that lacks the crystals of normal quartz

chemical formula: A representation of the atoms in a molecule

crystal: The result of a formation of atoms that follow a particular pattern

crystalline: Describing something with the nature of a crystal

cubic: Like a cube shape, with six sides

double terminated: Ends in a point on both sides

faceted: When a gemstone is cut with many flat surfaces

fluorescence: Property of some minerals where they give off a bright color when an ultraviolet light is shone on them

fortification banding: Parallel bands of color in an agate with sharp angular turns

geode: A cavity or hollow rock that is filled with crystals

glacier: A huge mass of slowly moving ice

hexagonal: A shape with six sides and six angles

igneous: A category of rocks that are volcanic in origin

inclusions: Small things that are trapped in a larger mass

lava: molten rock or magma that reaches the surface of the Earth

magma: Molten rock underneath the Earth

metamorphic: A category of rocks that have been changed by heat and pressure

molecule: A group of atoms that are bonded together

octahedral: A shape with 8 sides

ore: Rock that is mined for a particular mineral or element

organic: From or relating to a living organism

petrified wood: Fossilized wood, usually preserved by permineralization so that it has some of its original form

pocket: A hole or cavity in rock or an object

precipitate: To form or fall out of a liquid or gas solution

pseudomorph: A mineral that has replaced another mineral but kept the original shape

range: A line of mountains

rhyolite: A volcanic rock that is usually light colored

sedimentary: A category of rocks that is formed by deposition

silica: SiO_2, usually found as quartz

tabular: A flat tabletop shape

troy ounce: A unit of measure that is normally used to weigh gold or silver; slightly heavier than a standard ounce

volcanic: Originating in or relating to a volcano

weathering: The process of reducing a rock to smaller bits by the weather and erosion

zeolite: A group of minerals that usually are found in volcanic rocks but may also be found in places with evaporates

PLACES TO SEE GEMS AND MINERALS

Minerals can be found in every state, but the best places to see them are in museums and occasionally in special parks. While there are many museums and parks in every state, the ones listed here have minerals and gems on display or are generally related to geology. There are many more museums and parks not listed, so ask around! Be sure to check visiting hours and information before you go.

ALABAMA

Anniston Museum of Natural History (Anniston)
McWane Science Center (Birmingham)
Alabama Museum of Natural History (Tuscaloosa)

ALASKA

Alaska Museum of Science & Nature (Anchorage)
University of Alaska Museum of the North (Fairbanks)
Alaska State Museum (Juneau)

ARIZONA

Petrified Forest National Park
Bisbee Mining and Historical Museum (Bisbee)
Bisbee Queen Mine tour (Bisbee)
Pinal Geology & Mineral Museum (Coolidge)

Museum of Northern Arizona (Flagstaff)
Arizona Museum of Natural History (Mesa)
Arizona-Sonora Desert Museum (Tucson)
University of Arizona Mineral Museum (Tucson)

ARKANSAS

Arkansas State University Museum (Jonesboro)
Turner Neal Museum of Natural History and Pomeroy Planetarium (Monticello)
Crater of Diamonds State Park (Murfreesboro)
Matilda & Karl Pfeiffer Museum (Piggott)

CALIFORNIA

Humboldt State University Natural History Museum (Arcata)
Buena Vista Museum of Natural History & Science (Bakersfield)
Gateway Science Museum, California State University (Chico)
Fallbrook Gem & Mineral Museum (Fallbrook)
Children's Natural History Museum (Fremont)
Western Science Center (Hemet)
Natural History Museum Los Angeles County (Los Angeles)
California State Mining and Mineral Museum (Mariposa)
Pacific Grove Museum of Natural History (Pacific Grove)
Petaluma Wildlife & Natural Science Museum (Petaluma)
Maturango Museum (Ridgecrest)
World Museum of Natural History, La Sierra University (Riverside)
Sierra College Natural History Museum (Rocklin)
San Diego Natural History Museum (San Diego)
San Diego Mineral, Gem & Fossil Museum (San Diego)
California Academy of Science (San Francisco)
Santa Barbara Museum of Natural History (Santa Barbara)

COLORADO

Western Museum of Mining & Industry (Colorado Springs)
Underground Mining Museum (Creede)
Denver Museum of Nature & Science (Denver)
Colorado School of Mines Geology Museum (Golden)
National Mining Hall of Fame and Museum (Leadville)
Rocky Mountain Dinosaur Resource Center (Woodland Park)

CONNECTICUT

Bruce Museum (Greenwich)
Connecticut Museum of Mining and Mineral Science (Kent)
Yale Peabody Museum of Natural History (New Haven)

DELAWARE

University of Delaware Mineralogical Museum (Newark)
Delaware Museum of Natural History (Wilmington)

DISTRICT OF COLUMBIA

Smithsonian National Museum of Natural History

FLORIDA

Gillespie Museum (Deland)
Florida Museum of Natural History (Gainesville)

GEORGIA

Fernbank Museum of Natural History (Atlanta)
Tellus Science Museum (Cartersville)

HAWAII

Bernice Pauahi Bishop Museum (Honolulu)

IDAHO

Idaho Museum of Mining & Geology (Boise)
Orma J. Smith Museum of Natural History (Caldwell)
Idaho Museum of Natural History (Pocatello)

ILLINOIS
Field Museum of Natural History (Chicago)
Peggy Notebaert Nature Museum (Chicago)
Elgin Public Museum of Natural History & Anthropology (Elgin)
Lizzadro Museum of Lapidary Art (Elmhurst)
Burpee Museum of Natural History (Rockford)
Funk Prairie Home Museum (Shirley)
Illinois State Museum (Springfield)
Midwest Museum of Natural History (Sycamore)

INDIANA
Children's Museum of Indianapolis (Indianapolis)
Indiana State Museum (Indianapolis)
Joseph Moore Museum (Richmond)

IOWA
Putnam Museum and Science Center (Davenport)
University of Iowa Museum of Natural History (Iowa City)

KANSAS
Johnston Geology Museum (Emporia)
Galena Mining and Historical Museum (Galena)
KU Biodiversity Institute and Natural History Museum (Lawrence)
Keystone Gallery (Scott City)
Museum of World Treasures (Wichita)

KENTUCKY
Kentucky Science Center (Louisville)
Ben E. Clement Mineral Museum (Marion)

LOUISIANA
Louisiana Art & Science Museum (Baton Rouge)
Museum of Natural Science, Louisiana State University (Baton Rouge)
Lafayette Science Museum (Lafayette)

MAINE
Maine State Museum (Augusta)
Maine Mineral and Gem Museum (Bethel)
Nylander Museum (Caribou)

MARYLAND
Maryland Science Center (Baltimore)

MASSACHUSETTS
Beneski Museum of Natural History (Amherst)
Harvard Museum of Natural History (Cambridge)
Mineralogical & Geological Museum at Harvard University (Cambridge)
Berkshire Museum (Pittsfield)
Ecotarium (Worcester)

MICHIGAN
University of Michigan Museum of Natural History (Ann Arbor)
Kingman Museum (Battle Creek)
Cranbrook Institute of Science (Bloomfield Hills)
Wayne State University Geology Mineral Museum (Detroit)
Michigan State University Museum (East Lansing)
Quincy Mine Hoist Tours (Hancock)
A. E. Seaman Mineral Museum of Michigan Tech (Houghton)
Schmaltz Geology and Mineral Museum (Kalamazoo)
Central Michigan University Museum of Cultural and Natural History (Mount Pleasant)

MINNESOTA
Science Museum of Minnesota (St. Paul)

MISSISSIPPI
Dunn-Seiler Museum (Starkville)

MISSOURI
Joplin History & Mineral Museum (Joplin)

Richard L. Sutton Jr., MD, Museum of Geosciences (Kansas City)
St. Louis Science Center (St. Louis)

MONTANA
Montana Bureau of Mines & Geology Mineral Museum (Butte)

NEBRASKA
Agate Fossil Beds National Monument (Harrison)
Hastings Museum (Hastings)
University of Nebraska State Museum (Lincoln)

NEVADA
Nevada State Museum (Carson City)
Nevada State Museum (Las Vegas)
Las Vegas Natural History Museum (Las Vegas)
W. M. Keck Earth Science and Mineral Engineering Museum (Reno)

NEW HAMPSHIRE
Children's Museum of New Hampshire (Dover)
Little Nature Museum (Warner)

NEW JERSEY
Franklin Mineral Museum (Franklin)
Rutgers University Geology Museum (New Brunswick)
Morris Museum (Morristown)
Newark Museum (Newark)
Sterling Hill Mining Museum (Ogdensburg)
New Jersey State Museum (Trenton)

NEW MEXICO
New Mexico Museum of Natural History & Science (Albuquerque)
Sherman Dugan Museum of Geology (Farmington)
Las Cruces Museum of Nature & Science (Las Cruces)
Miles Mineral Museum (Portales)
New Mexico Bureau of Geology Museum (Socorro)

NEW YORK
New York State Museum (Albany)
Buffalo Museum of Science (Buffalo)
Museum of the Earth (Ithaca)
American Museum of Natural History (New York City)

NORTH CAROLINA
Asheville Museum of Science (Asheville)
Aurora Fossil Museum (Aurora)
Franklin Gem & Mineral Museum (Franklin)
Museum of Life + Science (Durham)
Schiele Museum of Natural History (Gastonia)
North Carolina Museum of Natural Sciences (Raleigh)
Museum of North Carolina Minerals (Spruce Pine)

NORTH DAKOTA
North Dakota Heritage Center & State Museum (Bismarck)
Dickinson Museum Center (Dickinson)

OHIO
Cincinnati Museum of Natural History & Science (Cincinnati)
Cleveland Museum of Natural History (Cleveland)
Orton Geological Museum, Ohio State University (Columbus)
Limper Geology Museum, Miami University (Oxford)

OKLAHOMA
Sam Noble Museum of Natural History (Norman)

OREGON
Rice Northwest Museum of Rocks and Minerals (Hillsboro)

PENNSYLVANIA
State Museum of Pennsylvania (Harrisburg)
Delaware County Institute of Science (Media)
Academy of Natural Sciences of Drexel University (Philadelphia)

Wagner Free Institute of Science (Philadelphia)
Carnegie Museum of Natural History (Pittsburgh)
Everhart Museum (Scranton)
Earth and Mineral Sciences Museum & Art Gallery (University Park)

RHODE ISLAND
Roger Williams Park Museum of Natural History (Providence)

SOUTH CAROLINA
Charleston Museum (Charleston)
Bob Campbell Geology Museum (Clemson)
McKissick Museum (Columbia)
South Carolina State Museum (Columbia)

SOUTH DAKOTA
Badlands National Park
Black Hills Institute of Geological Research (Hill City)
South Dakota School of Mines & Technology Geology Museum (Rapid City)
Journey Museum & Learning Center (Rapid City)

TENNESSEE
McClung Museum of Natural History & Culture (Knoxville)

TEXAS
Texas Memorial Museum (Austin)
Brazos Valley Museum of Natural History (Bryan)
Brazosport Museum of Natural Science (Chute)
Perot Museum of Nature and Science (Dallas)
Fort Worth Museum of Science and History (Fort Worth)
Houston Museum of Natural Science (Houston)
Heard Natural Science Museum & Wildlife Sanctuary (McKinney)
Permian Basin Petroleum Museum (Midland)
Mayborn Museum (Waco)

UTAH
Box Elder Museum of Natural History (Brigham City)
John Hutchings Museum of Natural History (Lehi)
Museum of Moab (Moab)
Natural History Museum of Utah (Salt Lake City)
Utah Field House of Natural History State Park Museum (Vernal)

VERMONT
Perkins Geology Museum at the University of Vermont (Burlington)
Vermont Museum of Mining and Minerals (Grafton)

VIRGINIA
Virginia Tech Museum of Geosciences (Blacksburg)
Virginia Museum of Natural History (Martinsville)

WASHINGTON
Burke Museum of Natural History and Culture (Seattle)

WEST VIRGINIA
West Virginia Geological & Economic Survey Museum (Morgantown)

WISCONSIN
Earthaven Museum (Gillette)
Kenosha Public Museum (Kenosha)
University of Wisconsin Geology Museum (Madison)
Weis Earth Science Museum (Menesha)

WYOMING
Tate Geological Museum (Casper)
University of Wyoming Geological Museum (Laramie)

FURTHER READING

To learn more about state fossils and paleontology in general, please check out the following books and websites:

Hankin, Rosie. *Rocks, Crystals, & Minerals*. Edison, NJ: Quintet Books, 2004.

Lyman, Kennie. *Gems and Precious Stones*. New York: Simon & Schuster, 1986.

McPherson, Alan. *State Geosymbols: Geological Symbols of the 50 United States*. Bloomington, IN: AuthorHouse, 2011.

Pellent, Chris. *Rocks and Minerals*. New York: Dorling Kindersley, 1992.

Staebler, Gloria A., and Wendell E. Wilson, eds. *American Mineral Treasures*. East Hampton, CO: Lithographie, 2008.

WEBSITES:

Mindat.org; Mines, Minerals, and More. http://Mindat.org"

Jeffrey A's Online Museum and Rock Shop. www.jagates.com

Michael Klimetz's science website. https://earthphysicsteaching.homestead.com/

Gold Rush Nuggets: gold and mineral hunting: www.goldrushnuggets.com/

Gator Girl Rocks: America's Best Rockhounding Resource. http://gatorgirlrocks.com/

Excalibur Mineral Corp. http://excaliburmineral.com/

Wikipedia entry about minerals. https://en.wikipedia.org/wiki/Mineral

50 States Guide. www.ereferencedesk.com/

PHOTO CREDITS

Introductory pages, diamond: Courtesy of Ron Ruschman, photo by Jeff Scovil

Alabama gem: Courtesy of the University of Alabama Museums, Tuscaloosa, AL

Alabama mineral: Courtesy of Michael P. Klimetz

Alaska mineral: Courtesy of Goldnuggetsforsale.com

Arizona mineral: Smithsonian Institution, CC0 license: www.si.edu/object/wulfenite:nmnhmineralsciences_1152986

Arkansas gem: Arkansas diamond: Smithsonian Institution, CC0 license: www.si.edu/objectdiamond:nmnhmineralsciences_1167604

California gem: Courtesy of Kyle Hunter, a.k.a. Benitoite Kid

California mineral: Courtesy of Goldnuggetsforsale.com

Connecticut cut gem: Courtesy of Missouri River Sapphire Company

Delaware mineral: Photo by author, specimen courtesy of Gene Hartstein

Hawaii gem rough: Courtesy of Putzu

Idaho gem: Courtesy of Huckleberry Garnets

Idaho mineral: Smithsonian Institution, CC0 license; www.si.edu/object/opal:nmnhmineralsciences_10209913

Illinois gem: Courtesy of Capistrano Mining Company, www.capistranominingcompany.com

Indiana gem and minerals: Courtesy of the Indiana State Museums and Historic Sites

Iowa gem: Courtesy of Jeffrey Anderson

Kansas gem: Courtesy of Glenn Rockers

Louisiana gem: LaPearlite®, courtesy of Anne Dale, GG, PG, FGA

Louisiana mineral: Specimen courtesy of James Green, Hammond, LA

Maryland gem: Specimen courtesy of Kimberly M. Reichart

Michigan mineral: Courtesy of anonymous

Minnesota gem: Courtesy of Jeffrey Anderson

Mississippi gem and mineral: Courtesy of James E. Starnes, RPG MDEQ, Mississippi Office of Geology

Missouri gem: Courtesy of Jeffrey Anderson

Missouri mineral calcite: Smithsonian Institution CC0: https://www.si.edu/object/calcite:nmnhmineralsciences_1082522

Nebraska gem: Courtesy of Jeffrey Anderson

Nevada gem cabochons: Courtesy of anonymous

Nevada turquoise: Courtesy of the Durango Silver Company, www.durangosilver.com

New Mexico mineral: Smithsonian Institution CC0: www.si.edu/object/smithsonite:nmnhmineralsciences_1080823

New York gem: Courtesy of the Barton Mines Corporation

North Carolina gem: Smithsonian Institution CC0: www.si.edu/object/beryl-var-emerald:nmnhmineralsciences_1082279

North Carolina mineral: Courtesy of Jasun McAvoy, www.mineralman.com

North Dakota mineral: Courtesy of John Krygier

Oregon gem: Smithsonian Institution CC0: www.si.edu/object/labradorite-var-sunstone:nmnhmineralsciences_11149733

Oregon mineral: Josephinite photo by author; oregonite, courtesy of Tony Nikischer

Pennsylvania gems: Courtesy of the collection of Kerry Matt; courtesy of bigstockphoto.com

Pennsylvania mineral: Courtesy of the collection of Kerry Matt

Rhode Island gems: Smithsonian Institution CC0: www.si.edu/object/quartz:nmnhmineralsciences_1166643

Rhode Island mineral: Courtesy of Museum of Natural History and Planetarium, Roger Williams Park

South Carolina gem: Courtesy of Rusty James

South Carolina mineral: Courtesy of Michael P. Klimetz

South Dakota gem: Courtesy of Anthony Lindgren

South Dakota minerals: Courtesy of Gary Olson

Tennessee gem: Courtesy of Robert Keast, www.birdsong.com

Tennessee mineral: Courtesy of Jeffrey Anderson

Texas gems: Specimen from Mason County Collectibles

Washington gem: Courtesy of Matt Heaton / Fossilera.com

West Virginia gems: Courtesy of E. Ray Garton, Prehistoric West Virginia

Wisconsin gems and mineral: Courtesy of William Cordua

Wyoming mineral: Courtesy of the Wyoming Mining Association

ACKNOWLEDGMENTS

This book would not have been possible without the recommendations, contacts, information, editing, and good will of the following people:

Susan Aber
Jeffrey Anderson
Kelly Arnold
Mathew Becker
Michael Bonafede
William Cordua
Anne Dale
Michael Dale
Trinity Daniels
Travis Deti
Janet Dunkelberger
Carrie Eaton
Peggy Fishkeller
John Friel
Nadine Gabriel
E. Ray Garton
Kim Grandizio
Tracy Hargrave Gray

James Green
Warren Grote
Joseph Hall
Dillon Hartman
Matt Heaton
Kyle Hunter
Rusty James
Robert Keast
Michael P. Klimetz
John Krygier
Hugo Laverde
Rachael Ledford
Jane Levy
Tony Lindgren
Mason County Collectibles
Kerry Matt
Maui Divers Jewelry
Jasun McAvoy

Mandy McAvoy
Ed C. Murphy
Tony Nikischer
Gary Olson
Alfredo Petrov
Mary B. Prondzinski
PuTzu
Jolyon Ralph
Kimberly M. Reichart
Ian Robertson
Glenn Rockers
Ron Ruschman

Wayne Schrimp
Nelson Shaffer
Jake Sheff
Jake Slagle
Seth Sorenson
Heather Spence
James E. Starnes
Frederick Watts
Andrew Wendruff
Joyce Wolf
Brandy Zzyzx
Justin Zzyzx

INDEX